Horus

BY VIRGINIA LOH-HAGAN

Gods and goddesses were the main characters of myths. Myths are traditional stories from ancient cultures. Storytellers answered questions about the world by creating exciting explanations. People thought myths were true. Myths explained the unexplainable. They helped people make sense of human behavior and nature. Today, we use science to explain the world. But people still love myths. Myths may not be literally true. But they have meaning. They tell us something about our history and culture.

45th Parallel Press

Published in the United States of America by Cherry Lake Publishing
Ann Arbor, Michigan
www.cherrylakepublishing.com

Reading Adviser: Marla Conn, MS, Ed., Literacy specialist, Read-Ability, Inc.
Book Design: Jen Wahi

Photo Credits: ©Howard David Johnson, 2019, cover, 1, 19; ©Lund Dahl Photo/Shutterstock, 5; ©Babin/Shutterstock, 6; ©Rémih/Wikimedia/Creative Commons Attribution-Share Alike 3.0 Unported, 8; ©Calin Stan/Shutterstock, 11; ©Mikadun/Shutterstock, 13; ©Jose Ignacio Soto/Shutterstock, 15; ©agsaz/Shutterstock, 17; ©maradon 333/Shutterstock, 21; ©Airijo/Shutterstock, 23; ©amin esmat .jordan/Shutterstock, 24; ©Goddard_Photography/iStock, 27; ©Johan Cronje/Shutterstock, 29

45th Parallel Press is an imprint of Cherry Lake Publishing.

Library of Congress Cataloging-in-Publication Data

Names: Loh-Hagan, Virginia, author. | Loh-Hagan, Virginia. Gods & goddesses of the ancient world.
Title: Horus / Written by Virginia Loh-Hagan.
Description: Ann Arbor, Michigan : Cherry Lake Publishing, 2019. | Series: Gods and goddesses of the ancient world
Identifiers: LCCN 2019004185 | ISBN 9781534147713 (hardcover) | ISBN 9781534149144 (pdf) | ISBN 9781534150577 (pbk.) | ISBN 9781534152007 (hosted ebook)
Subjects: LCSH: Horus (Egyptian deity)—Juvenile literature. | Gods, Egyptian—Juvenile literature. | Mythology, Egyptian—Juvenile literature.
Classification: LCC BL2450.H6 L64 2019 | DDC 299/.312113—dc23
LC record available at https://lccn.loc.gov/2019004185

Printed in the United States of America
Corporate Graphics

ABOUT THE AUTHOR:

Dr. Virginia Loh-Hagan is an author, university professor, former classroom teacher, and curriculum designer. Horus is a hawk god. There are three hawks that circle Virginia's backyard. She lives in San Diego with her very tall husband and very naughty dogs. To learn more about her, visit www.virginialoh.com.

TABLE OF CONTENTS

CHAPTER 1

FALCON GOD

Who is Horus? What does he look like? Who are his parents?

Horus was an **ancient** Egyptian god. Ancient means old. Egypt is a country in the Middle East. It's in North Africa.

Ancient Egyptians honored Horus. Horus was the god of sky. He was the god of kings. He was the god of wars. He had a **falcon** head. Falcons are birds of prey. They have powerful beaks and claws. They're strong hunters. Horus was an important god.

Horus wore a crown. His crown had a cobra. Cobras are snakes with hoods. Sometimes, Horus had the body of a lion. But most times, he had the body of a man.

 Horus was probably connected with the peregrine falcon.

Ancient Egyptian gods married their own family members. Isis and Osiris were also brother and sister.

Horus's name means "the one who is above." It also means "the **distant** one." Distant means far away. As a godly falcon, Horus was in the air. He flew around. He was everywhere.

Horus's parents were Osiris and Isis. They're the most important Egyptian gods. They were **creator gods**. Creator gods made the world. Osiris was the god of the

Family Tree

Grandparents: Geb (god of the earth) and Nut (goddess of the sky)

Parents: Osiris (god of the dead and rebirth) and Isis (goddess of marriage, fertility, motherhood, magic, and medicine)

Brother: Anubis (god of embalming)

Wife: Serket (goddess of fertility, nature, animals, medicine, and magic) and/or Hathor (mistress of sky and stars)

Children: Imset (protector of liver and guardian of the south), Hapi (protector of lungs and guardian of the north), Duamutef (protector of the stomach and guardian of the east), and Qebehsenuef (protector of the intestines and guardian of the west), and Thoth (god of wisdom)

underworld. The underworld is the place where dead people's souls live. Isis was the goddess of marriage, motherhood, magic, and medicine. Isis and Osiris loved each other. Osiris ruled the world. Isis became his queen.

Set was the god of **chaos**. Chaos means disorder. Set became jealous. He wanted power. He killed Osiris. He hacked Osiris's body into many pieces. He scattered his body parts all over. Isis became a bird. She found most of Osiris's body parts. She used magic. She brought Osiris back to life. She gave birth to Horus.

Isis had to protect Horus from Set. Set tried to kill Horus. He sent dangerous animals. He sent floods. He sent fires. Set did whatever he could to kill Horus. But Isis wouldn't let anything happen to Horus. She hid him by the Nile River. She took care of him.

 Set was the brother of Isis and Osiris.

CHAPTER 2

PROTECTOR OF PHARAOHS

What happens between Horus and Set? How is Horus connected to the ancient Egyptian rulers?

Horus was born to **avenge** his father's death. Avenge means to punish. Horus grew up. He learned to fight off danger. He became a strong fighter. Isis told him to protect the people of Egypt. She told him to take back his father's throne. Set was a bad ruler. He liked violence. The people needed peace.

Horus and Set fought for 80 years. They had many battles. Isis helped Horus. She used magic to help win battles. In some stories, it's believed she felt bad for Set. She didn't help Horus. This made Horus mad. Horus cut off her head. But Isis used magic. She grew a cow's head. She forgave Horus. Horus forgave her.

Horus is known to be a good son.

All in the Family

Serket was an Egyptian goddess. In some stories, she married Horus. She was often connected with scorpions. Her name means "she who tightens the throat." She was known to sting and bite. But she also healed and cured. In images, she's shown as a woman with a scorpion head. She's shown with open arms. This means she protected others. Ancient Egyptians were scared of scorpions. Scorpion stings were common. Female scorpions were larger than males. They had more poison. Their stings caused a lot of pain. They stopped people from breathing. They killed little children. People believed Serket was responsible for scorpions. This made her important. People wore jewelry with her name. They did this to protect themselves. Serket kept women safe when they had children. In some stories, she protected Isis when she gave birth to Horus. Serket was worshipped by doctors. Some ancient Egyptian doctors were called the "followers of Serket."

Set was the god of deserts and foreign lands.

Horus and Set dared each other a lot. They had a boat race.
They each agreed to use a boat of stone. Horus tricked Set.
He cheated. His boat was made of wood. He painted it to
look like stone. Set's boat sank. Horus won. He was made
the **victor**. Victors are winners.

Horus and Set made a deal. They divided the land. Horus took
back his father's throne. He ruled the areas around the Nile
River. He ruled the earth. Set ruled over the deserts. He lived
in the sky. But Horus was the main ruler. He ruled over Set.

Horus became known as the "**uniter** of lands." To unite means to join. Horus joined lands and people together. He restored order. He brought peace. He avenged wrongs. He punished crimes. He ruled wisely. He ruled with Isis's help. He became the protector of **pharaohs**. Pharaohs are ancient Egyptian rulers.

Horus was a symbol for **divine** power. Divine means godly. Horus was the first divine king of Egypt. Ruling pharaohs were believed to be Horus. Every new pharaoh was called a "living Horus." They said their power came from Horus. They said Horus ruled through them.

Isis became known as the "mother of pharaohs."

CHAPTER 3

LIFE OR DEATH?

How is Horus immortal? What are some stories about Horus's death?

When pharaohs died, they changed form. They changed from Horus to Osiris. Osiris ruled the **afterlife**. Afterlife is life after death. It's the next world. Pharaohs were still godly in death. They ruled the kingdom of dead people's souls.

Horus moved into the form of the next pharaoh. He was **immortal**. Immortal means living forever. Ancient Egypt lasted over 3,000 years. There were about 170 pharaohs.

Horus lived through all these pharaohs. In this way, he never died. He was **reincarnated**. Reincarnated means coming back to life after dying in another body. This all means that pharaohs inherited erternal life. Eternal means forever.

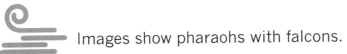

Images show pharaohs with falcons.

There were other stories about Horus dying. In one story, Horus was on a cross. He was nailed to it. He was buried for 3 days. Then, he came back to life.

In another story, he became Ra. Ra is the Sun God. Horus died every night. He came back to life every morning. This happened when the sun rose.

In yet another story, Horus was killed. Like his father, his body was chopped into bits. He was thrown into the river. Isis helped. She used her magic. She got a crocodile to fish him out. She put Horus back together.

 Other falcon gods were Month, Sokar, and Ra. Month was the god of war. Sokar was a god of death. Ra was the god of the sun.

CHAPTER 4

THE EYES ARE WATCHING!

What is the "Eye of Horus"? What are Horus's symbols? Who are Horus's sons?

As a falcon, Horus was the master of the sky. His right eye was the sun. His left eye was the moon. Horus flew across the sky. He created night and day. He also flew to protect his people. Horus's eyes were powerful.

The "Eye of Horus" was a symbol. It was on **amulets**. Amulets are jewelry. They could be necklaces. They're like lucky charms. They protect against evil and danger. They protect people. They heal.

The "Eye of Horus" was always watching. It protected the world from chaos. It protected pharaohs in the afterlife.

Horus was also called Horus in the Horizon. The horizon is the line where the earth and sky appear to meet. Horus was connected to the rising sun. He was connected to dawn. In this way, he saw everything. He wore a sun disc **headdress**. A headdress is a head covering. Sun discs are large circles.

The "Eye of Horus" symbol was found in King Tut's tomb.

Real World Connection

Horus isn't the only person with a falcon head. Freddie Falcon is an official mascot. Mascots are symbols. They represent a group. They are supposed to bring good luck. Freddie Falcon represents the Atlanta Falcons. The Atlanta Falcons are a football team in Georgia. They're part of the National Football League (NFL). It's someone's job to wear the Freddie Falcon costume. Freddie Falcon was Atlanta's first mascot. He's entertained fans for over 35 years. He goes to games. He goes to parties. He goes to shows. He goes to weddings. He goes to meetings. He goes to all kinds of events. He's been to many cities. He's been to New York City. He's been to Los Angeles. He's even been overseas. He goes to military bases. He's been to Cuba. He's been to Egypt. He's been to Hong Kong. He was a part of the Chinese New Year day parade.

Horus was connected to the cross symbol.

Horus was often shown with his wings stretched out. This showed how he watched over all. His main weapon was a **scepter**. Scepters are long sticks. They have fancy designs. They're a symbol of power. Horus's scepter had a falcon head on the top. He used it in his war against Set.

Horus had 4 sons. His sons were Imset, Hapi, Duamutef, and Qebehsenuef. Imset was a human. He guarded the south. Hapi was a baboon. He guarded the north.

Horus may have had many wives.

Duamutef was a jackal. He guarded the east. Qebehsenuef was a hawk. He guarded the west. Together, they watched all the world. Some stories also say that Thoth, god of wisdom, was Horus's child.

Ancient Egyptians thought royal bodies should be saved. They turned dead bodies into **mummies**. Mummies are wrapped bodies. People's organs are taken out of their bodies. These organs are saved in special jars.

Horus's 4 sons protected organs. Imset protected livers. Hapi protected lungs. Duamutef protected stomachs. Qebehsenuef protected intestines. Intestines are tubes that carry food out from stomachs.

Cross-Cultural Connection

Ancient Egyptians believed a pharaoh's power came from gods. Ancient Chinese people believed the same. They believed in the "mandate of Heaven." Mandate means an order. Heaven was the home of the gods. China's early rulers got power from Heaven. This meant Heaven chose them to rule. These leaders ruled on Heaven's behalf. If leaders were bad, Heaven would punish them. Heaven would create bad events like fires and floods. It would also make leaders lose in wars. This meant a new leader was needed. The first Chinese ruler to have the "mandate of Heaven" was King Wen. Wen ruled the Zhou dynasty. A dynasty is a ruling family. When he was king, 5 planets lined up in the sky. This happened in 1059 BCE.

CHAPTER 5

FIGHT! FIGHT!

What are some stories about Horus's battles?

Horus won the war against Set. But their battles were painful. They both got hurt. Set hurt Horus. He attacked his right eye. This caused a solar eclipse. Solar eclipses are when the moon blocks out the sun's light. This is why the sun is hidden.

In another battle, Set hurt Horus's left eye. This is why the moon has **phases**. Moon phases are different shapes. This is also why the moon isn't as bright as the sun.

In yet another battle, Set tore out Horus's eye. He broke it into 6 pieces. The pieces represent a sense. Senses include touch, taste, hearing, thought, sight, and smell.

Horus and Set had **contests**. Contests are like dares. Horus and Set turned themselves into hippos. They wanted to see who could stay under water the longest.

Ancient Egyptians loved and feared hippos. Hippos live in the Nile River. The Nile River was the source of life.

Other gods helped fix Horus's eyes.

Explained By Science

Horus was believed to make wind. But science tells us a different story. Wind is a big movement of air. Air is made of molecules. Molecules are tiny bits of gases. They move very quickly. They crash into each other. They also crash into things on Earth. Air pressure is the amount of force these molecules push into an area. A lot of air molecules means more air pressure. Wind is caused by differences in air pressure. Air moves from high to low pressure areas. This makes winds of different speeds. Wind gets energy from the sun. The sun makes warm spots. It makes cool spots. Sea wind happens when land heats up on sunny days. This makes the air warm. Air rises. Cooler air from the sea rushes in. This makes wind. This wind blows for miles. Land wind happens at night. The land is cold. The sea is warmer than the land. Cool and warm air meet. This makes wind.

Hippos kill more people in Africa than any other large animals.

Hippos are powerful. But they're also dangerous. They attack. They run faster than humans over short distances. They ram into things. They represent chaos. People hunted hippos. Even pharaohs hunted hippos. This is like Horus winning over Set.

Don't anger the gods. Horus was very wise. He had great powers. And he knew how to use them.

- EgyptAir is an airline company. It started in 1932. It has a falcon on its logo. The falcon stands for Horus. Logo is a company symbol. (Horus is on many symbols in Egypt. He's on hotels. He's on restaurants.)

- Some people confused Horus with Nekheny. Nekheny was another falcon god. He was worshipped at Nekhen. Nekhen was the city of the falcon.

- The Narmer Palette is an Egyptian engraving. It's over 2 feet (61 centimeters) tall. It's shaped like a shield. It has a picture of Horus. Horus is in the form of a falcon. It's from 3100 BCE.

- In Greek myths, Horus is identified with Apollo. Apollo is the god of the arts. He is the protector of the young.

- Edfu is a city in Egypt. It's located on the Nile River. It's famous for having the Temple of Horus. The temple was built starting in around 237 BCE. It's still there today. Of all the ruins, it's the most intact.

- Some people connect Horus to Jesus Christ. Both their mothers gave birth to them in a special way. Both men are connected with a cross symbol.

- In some images, Horus is naked. He's on his mother's knee. Horus also appears on amulets. He protects against dangerous animals. Examples are lions, crocodiles, and snakes.

- Pharaohs wore black eyeliner. They made their eyes look like ovals. This made them look more like Horus.

- Ancient Egyptian sailors painted the "Eye of Horus" on their boats. This was to ward off storms. It was to protect sailors. It helped them travel safely.

CONSIDER THIS!

TAKE A POSITION! Some people think Horus is the most important Egyptian god. Do you agree or disagree? Argue your point with reasons and evidence. (Learn more about Egyptian gods and goddesses.)

SAY WHAT? Read the 45th Parallel Press book about Isis. How are Horus and Isis connected? Explain their relationship. Is it a good or bad relationship? Explain why you think so.

THINK ABOUT IT! Horus lived as all the pharaohs. That connected government and religion. In many places, the two are connected. But the United States believes in separation of church and state. What does this mean? Why would leaders want to connect themselves to God? What are the benefits? What are the issues?

LEARN MORE

Braun, Eric. *Egyptian Myths*. North Mankato, MN: Capstone Press, 2019.

McIntee, David, and Mark Stacey (illust.). *The War of Horus and Set*. Oxford: Osprey, 2013.

Napoli, Donna Jo, and Christina Balit (illust.). *Treasury of Egyptian Mythology: Classic Stories of Gods, Goddesses, Monsters, and Mortals*. Washington, DC: National Geographic Kids, 2013.

GLOSSARY

afterlife (AF-tur-life) life after death

amulets (AM-yoo-lets) jewelry used as good luck charms

ancient (AYN-shuhnt) old, from a long time ago

avenge (uh-VENJ) to get revenge in order to punish for a crime

chaos (KAY-ahs) disorder

contests (KAHN-tests) dares or challenges

creator gods (kree-AY-tur GAHDZ) gods who created the world and humans

distant (DIS-tuhnt) far away

divine (dih-VINE) godly

falcon (FAL-kuhn) bird of prey

headdress (HED-dres) a head covering

immortal (ih-MOR-tuhl) living forever

mummies (MUHM-eez) process of wrapping dead bodies to preserve them

pharaohs (FAIR-ohz) ancient Egyptian rulers

phases (FAZE-iz) shapes of a moon

reincarnated (ree-in-KAR-nay-ted) a body that has died and returned in another body

scepter (SEP-tur) a staff or fancy stick used to symbolize power

underworld (UHN-dur-wurld) the land of the dead

uniter (yoo-NITE-ur) a person who unites or joins people and places together

victor (VIK-tur) winner

INDEX